Spotlight on
Prehistoric
People

Tim Wood

Franklin Watts

London · New York · Sydney · Toronto

© 1988 Franklin Watts

Franklin Watts
12a Golden Square
London W1

First published in the USA by
Franklin Watts Inc.
387 Park Avenue South
New York, N.Y. 10016

Franklin Watts Australia
14 Mars Road
Lane Cove
NSW 2066

Phototypeset by Keyspools
Limited
Printed in Hong Kong

UK ISBN: 0 86313 686 9
US ISBN: 0–531–10541–5
Library of Congress Catalog
Card Number: 87–51475

Illustrations:
Eagle Artists
Christopher Forsey
Hayward Art Group
Michael Roffe
Bernard Long

Photographs:
Imitor

Design:
Janet King
David Jefferis

Technical consultant:
Anne Millward PhD

Note: The majority of
illustrations in this book
originally appeared in
Prehistoric Man,
An Easy-Read Fact Book.

Contents

Our early ancestors

Our ancestors were ape-like creatures called *Ramapithecus.* They lived in forests about 14 million years ago. They slept in the trees but came down on to the ground to feed. They learned to stand on their back legs to reach up for food.

The first man-apes

About 3 million years ago man-apes called hominids (the word *homo* means man) lived in Africa. They began to move out of the forests on to the grassy plains. There were several different kinds of hominids. One sort was *Australopithecus* or "southern apes."

Australopithecus eating ant grubs.

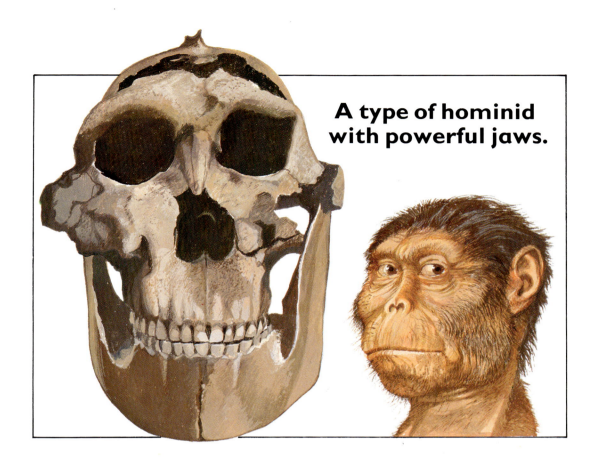

A type of hominid with powerful jaws.

Their brains were half the size of ours. They were only one and a half metres tall but they walked upright. Most hominids were vegetarians. They gathered and ate plants, fruit and birds' eggs. Other hominids may have hunted slow-moving animals.

7

The first toolmakers

About 2 million years ago a new hominid appeared in East Africa. Scientists called it *Homo habilis,* which means "handy man."

Like their ancestors they gathered fruits and berries, but they were also meat eaters. *Homo habilis* also had stronger hands and made simple stone tools.

Ape   **Human**

Apes and humans have similar hands.
The human thumb is longer. This allows
us to grip objects and use them with skill.

Prehistoric tools

The first human tools were made of flint, a stone that splits easily. It took many hours to chip a piece of flint into the correct shape.

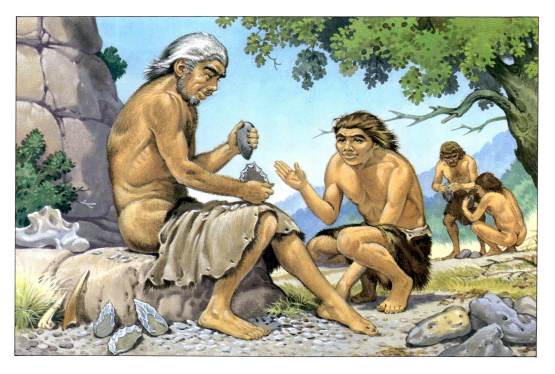

Young people learned the skills of tool-making from the older members of the group.

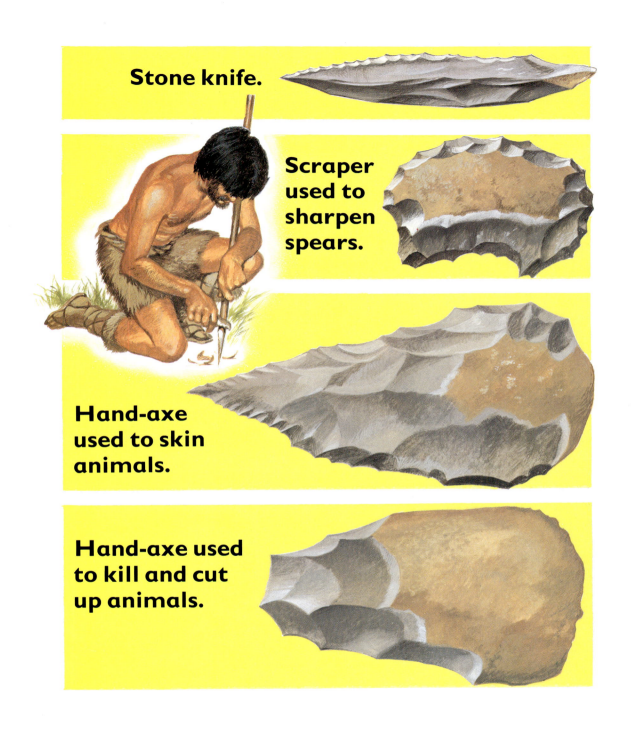

Stone knife.

Scraper used to sharpen spears.

Hand-axe used to skin animals.

Hand-axe used to kill and cut up animals.

*These tools are shown life-size.

Somewhere to live

Simple shelters like this kept *Homo habilis* warm and safe.

Homo habilis belonged to a larger group called *Homo erectus,* or "upright man." These hominids spread from Africa into Europe and Asia. They lived and hunted in groups. They built shelters. It seems likely that they had a language which made teamwork easier.

A shelter by the seashore.
There were lots of fish and
wild animals to catch here.

Conquest of fire

Control of fire was one of the most
important steps in human history.
Fire provided heat, light and
protection. Burning branches from
forest fires were used to light
the first camp-fires.

Thousands of years passed before humans discovered how to make fire. So they tried to keep the camp-fire going all the time. They learned how to cook meat in the flames.

15

The long winter

During the Ice Ages the cold weather killed off *Homo erectus.* They were replaced by *Homo sapiens,* or "wise" men. One group of these was called Neanderthals.

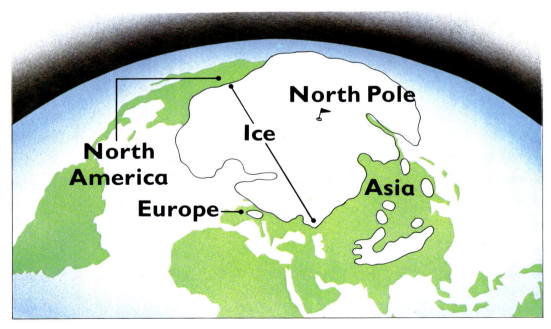

The world in the last Ice Age, 70,000 years ago

Neanderthal hunters

They lived in caves. They hunted wolves, bears and woolly mammoths. They used the thick furs of these animals as warm clothes and bedding.

Cave painters

The first really "modern" people appeared about **40,000** years ago. They were called **Cro-Magnon** after the place in France where their remains were found. Cro-Magnon people lived in big groups and were the world's first artists. They had better tools and weapons than **Neanderthals**, who died out.

Cro-Magnon cave painters.

They painted on the walls in the deepest, darkest parts of their caves. Perhaps the paintings were supposed to bring luck to the hunters. The paints were made from different-coloured earth mixed with water. Soot was used for black. Stone lamps which burned animal fat lit the caves.

A mammoth hunt

Cro-Magnons hunted mammoths during the Ice Ages. It took many people, using only spears and 20 stones, to kill a huge animal like a

mammoth. It provided them with meat for food, skin for clothes and tusks to build shelters. 21

Cro-Magnon skills

Sewing with leather thread using a bone needle.

Cro-Magnons were skillful workers. They used bone needles to sew together animal skins for clothes. They made jewellery out of pebbles, shells and fish bones. They improved weapons by adding barbs to spears and arrows.

Necklaces. One is made from fish bones, the other from sea shells.

Bone fish hooks.

A special harpoon (spear) for hunting deer. The head comes off and the pointed barbs keep it firmly in the animal. The hunter keeps hold of the handle and the rope.

The first farmers

About 10,000 years ago our ancestors found that if they planted wild seeds, then young plants would grow. They tamed goats, sheep, cattle and pigs. People became farmers. Instead of moving about, they stayed in one place to look after their crops and animals.

A farming village 10,000 years ago.

24

25

Finding out about the past

The earliest human remains have been found in East Africa.

Scientists think the earliest people lived in Africa. From here they spread over the rest of the world. Scientists have learned about prehistoric life by finding fossil remains of ancient plants, people and animals.

Scientists uncovering fossils.

27

The evolution of human beings

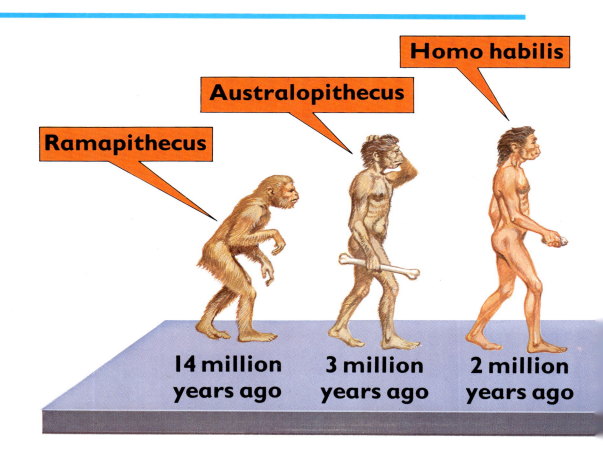

Ramapithecus

Australopithecus

Homo habilis

14 million years ago

3 million years ago

2 million years ago

We do not know the complete story of the evolution of human beings because few human fossils have been found.

The six main steps along the path from early hominid to modern human which are shown in this book.

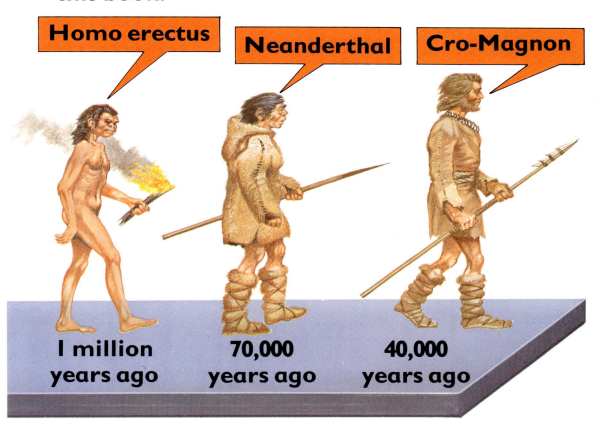

Homo erectus

Neanderthal

Cro-Magnon

I million years ago

70,000 years ago

40,000 years ago

Modern humans are four times heavier than *Ramapithecus* and have a brain which is now nearly four times bigger.

29

Prehistoric people facts

The earliest known shelter made by humans about 2 million years ago was found in Tanzania, Africa. All that is left is a circle of stones.

The oldest footprints in the world were found in Tanzania, Africa. They are thought to be almost 4 million years old. They were made by two adults and a child, and look exactly like footprints made by humans today.

Neanderthals had bigger brains than modern humans, though this does not mean they were more intelligent.

Neanderthals were the first people to bury their dead with ceremony. Fossil flower seeds found at a grave in a cave in Iraq show that flowers like hollyhocks and cornflowers had been placed round the body of a Neanderthal man.

No evidence of very early humans has been found in either North or South America. Scientists believe that the first Americans must have walked across a land bridge from Asia about 30,000 years ago. The ancestors of the American Indians were already *Homo sapiens.*

How to say the names

Cro-Magnon
crow-MAG-non

Hominid
HOM-in-id

Homo erectus
Ho-mo ee-REK-tuss

Homo habilis
Ho-mo HABY-liss

Homo sapiens
Ho-mo SAP-ee-enz

Australopithecus
oss-trall-oh-PITHY-kuss

Ramapithecus
Raa-maa-PITHY-kuss

Glossary

Here is the meaning of some of the words used in this book.

Ancestors
Members of your family who lived a long time before you.

Australopithecus
An early hominid. Its remains have been found in Africa.

Cro-Magnon
People who lived about 40,000 years ago. They looked similar to modern Europeans.

Evolution
The slow change and improvement which takes place in humans, animals and plants over millions of years.

Flint
A hard stone which splits easily and so is good for making tools and weapons.

Hominid
Ape-like ancestors of humans.

Homo erectus
Our ancestors who lived between 1 million and 250,000 years ago.

Homo habilis
Tool-making humans who were an early kind of *Homo erectus.*

Homo sapiens
Modern humans.

Neanderthal
A type of *Homo sapiens* which lived in the Ice Ages.

Prehistoric
Before written records were kept.

Ramapithecus
A small ape-like creature that may have been our ancestor.

31

Index